ADDIE GOES TO CHINA

BONNIE GATES WINDLE

Addie Goes to China

ISBN 978-1-940645-81-0

COURIER PUBLISHING

Greenville, South Carolina

PRINTED IN THE UNITED STATES OF AMERICA

PRAISE FOR *ADDIE GOES TO CHINA*

Reading *Addie Goes to China* is like taking a walk on memory lane for me. I knew Addie Cox when I was a little girl growing up in China and thought she was a tiny dynamo. In later years, I learned she was a dynamo indeed, one who left a shining trail of hope and love in her train. She even played Cupid in my and my husband's courtship some sixty years ago and forever holds a special place in our hearts. I'm thrilled to see Addie's story shared, so that those who love missions can learn of the ministry and courage of a tiny little woman who braved the unknown for the sake of sharing the good news.

*Rosalie Hall Hunt — Missionaries' kid
from China, emeritus IMB missionary
and author of books on pioneering women
of missions, including, most recently,* Out of Exile:
Fannie Heck & the Rest of the Story

Addie Cox is a heroine of the Christian faith. Her courage and conviction helped spread the Gospel in China, even at the risk of her own life. Some of her adventures are so dramatic that they remind us of the Apostle Paul. Bonnie Windle has done us a great service by getting the story into this fine book. The story of "Miss Addie" can inspire people of any age to give their lives to Jesus and follow wherever He leads.

Dr. Thrath C. Curry — Educator, Sunday school teacher, and friend of "Miss Addie"
(Author's note: Dr. Curry has been one of the people keeping alive the memory of Addie Cox for over fifty years, and she collaborated in the project to compile the stories of her life and work.)

Shortly after I arrived as the new pastor, I heard her name. I would soon learn her history. Addie Cox, a missionary to China for decades, was raised in the very church I now served! Somehow, that intimate connection made the mission of God more vibrant and real to me. I am so glad that

Bonnie Windle has taken the time and effort to publish this book about Addie's incredible life and ministry. I pray that as you read it, the mission of God will become more vibrant and real to you as well.

Ben Styles — Pastor of Carrollton Baptist Church from 1993-2000

INTRODUCTION

It is my desire to share about the life and work of Addie Estelle Cox, a friend of my grandmother, Cecil Harper Gates. The more I know about Addie's work, the more I appreciate her and what she and others have done in going to other countries and other cultures to share about the love of Jesus. It was my pleasure to know her when I was a young girl, as she visited our church during furloughs back to the States. Her bundle of energy, her serious commitment to sharing God's Word, and the discipline that was obvious in her life made an impression upon my life. May her memory and her devotion to Jesus be kept alive in the generations to come, and may God use this book to call out other people to mission fields still "ripe unto harvest."

— Bonnie Gates Windle

TABLE OF CONTENTS

ADDIE GOES TO CHINA

CHAPTER 1

A SMALL, QUIET COMMUNITY

On October 24, 1885, a little girl was born to John Wyley Cox and Frances Roan Eddins Cox in Providence, a small rural community in Pickens County, Alabama. She was the seventh child born to her family and was named Addie Estelle Cox.

Addie had two sisters, Pattie and Clara, and four brothers, Edward, Roy, Samuel, and Clayton. Addie was a small child with a beautiful smile and dark piercing eyes.

Her family moved to the small town of Carrollton when Addie was very young. The home they moved to had originally been constructed of logs, a one-story pioneer style home built in the mid-1860s. When her family moved to that home, they remodeled it into a two-story Victorian-style house. Porches extended the length of the house on both the lower and upper floors, and there was a beautiful decorative railing on the second-floor balcony.

The town of Carrollton offered many things that would be helpful to Addie. It had an academy where children could go and learn, a church within walking distance of her home, and close friends and neighbors to encourage her.

The town was located on a highway going to nearby large cities. It had a train that traveled to distant places. It was the gathering place for people from nearby communities as they came to take part in county government, pay their taxes, and be a part of community life. Much of this same community spirit would go with Addie as she went around the world telling others about Jesus.

Addie is on her way!

Addie's home

CHAPTER 2

GROWING UP

As the youngest member of her family, Addie was a curious child, interested in all the things going on around her. She enjoyed learning and wanted to keep pace with her older brothers and sisters. Addie attended the Carrollton male and female academy known as the "Curry House." There she learned reading, writing, and arithmetic in earlier grades and, later, algebra, geometry, trigonometry, Latin, Greek, and music. She began to observe more and more of the world around her. She was quick to learn, and she remembered these things from her home in Carrollton when she later shared them with Chinese children around the world.

I can imagine Addie as a small child, and later as a teenager, enjoying the porches on her family's home. From there, she was able to see and learn about the nature of God, to listen to the birds, and to see the seasons changing.

God was at work in Addie's world (as He works in our world today). He had placed her in a Christian home, where she was loved by her parents and her sisters (Pattie and Clara) and her brothers (Edward, Roy, Samuel, and Clayton). She learned about the love of God from her family, at church, and from the events that happened in her life.

Carrollton Male and Female Academy

CHAPTER 3

ADDIE INVITES JESUS INTO HER HEART

Addie loved her church and enjoyed the short walk from her home to church. At any time of the year, it was a beautiful walk, and Addie could appreciate all the things that God had created. She could see the trees, hear the birds, and smell the flowers, and she knew that the world God created was good.

At the age of thirteen, Addie invited Jesus into her heart and was baptized at her church. From that time on, she was eager to know Jesus more and to serve Him in her life.

Addie could do many things, and she did them well. She helped to organize the ladies in mission groups. She was talented in music and played the piano. She gave a piano concert at her church and gave money from the concert to mission projects.

She worked with mission projects in churches

nearby, and her fine work was recognized and honored by the local group of churches.

During her early years, the role of women in the church was limited. A woman was highly respected and honored by men but not allowed to have public responsibility or to speak publicly to a congregation of men and women. But by the 1900s opinion was changing, and by 1904 Addie was elected by her local Union Baptist Association as vice president of the Woman's Missionary Union. In this role, she would assist her pastor.

In 1904, at the age of nineteen, Addie graduated from Alabama Central Female College in Tuscaloosa. She taught school at the college for six years. Then she taught school in Pickens County and in Tuscaloosa County.

In 1913, at the age of twenty-eight, Addie earned a Baptist Missionary Training degree at the WMU Training School in Louisville, Kentucky.

Addie is preparing to go to the Mission Field!

Carrollton Baptist Church circa 1946

Congregation of Carrollton Baptist Church, 1946

21

Addie's Bible

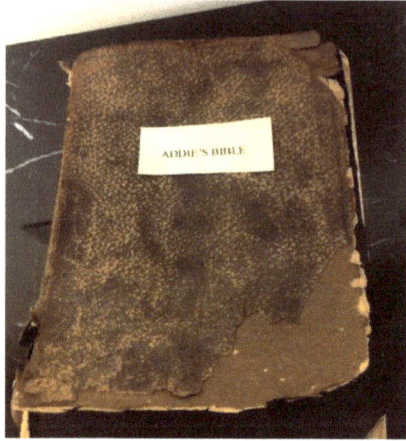

Alabama Central Female College

CHAPTER 4

THE BIG CITY

After her schooling, our beloved Addie moved to the big city of Birmingham in 1913. There she began work as the pastor's assistant at the First Baptist Church of Birmingham. That experience gave her a broader view of God's Kingdom work, especially in the area of missions. God used her talents of music, missions, and loving people as He continued to prepare her for the great work ahead.

The world opened for Addie, and she saw more and more of the world God had created — from the small rural community where she was born, to a larger community, to the city of Tuscaloosa, and then to Birmingham, the largest city in Alabama.

It wasn't long before Addie began to work with missions over the state of Alabama. On July 11, 2018, Addie was appointed by the Foreign Mission Board of the Southern Baptist Convention (the agency is now called the International Mission Board, or IMB) to serve as a missionary to the interior of China.

Addie is really on her way!

How excited she must have been, because she knew early that God was calling her to the mission field. She had prepared well. Now she was on her way.

Can you imagine the joy and excitement that Addie must have felt? What clothes would she carry? What books? What personal things from home would she take with her to another part of the world? Addie had all these decisions to make, knowing that she could carry only a small part of her world from Alabama. Most of what she carried with her, she carried in her heart and in her mind.

Addie would miss her family, but she would write to them often from China. They would also write to her and keep her in touch with family during the seven years she would serve before coming home for a furlough.

Addie as a young woman

Student body, Tuscaloosa Female Academy, 1912-13
(Addie is at front center)

25

CHAPTER 5

ON THE BOAT TO CHINA

Addie traveled by boat, the S.S. Monteagle, from California to China. Airplane travel was not available then, and people traveled by boat. In those days, travel to another country was a long and tiring journey.

A typewriter was one of the things that Addie carried to China with her. On the boat, it was crated and packed in her trunk, and she wrote handwritten letters to her family telling them about her travel.

In a letter to her nephew John, written on September 6, 1918, from the boat in the Pacific Ocean, Addie said she was having a splendid voyage. They were due to arrive at Yokohama, Japan, the next night; at Shanghai, China, eight days later; and then at Peking, China, by train about October 1.

In her letter to John, Addie copied Scriptures

from the New Testament. She suggested that in later letters she would give him Scripture references and let him look up at the verses.

Addie was teaching others about Jesus even as she wrote letters to her family.

Addie is really on her way!

The Monteagle

Addie's typewriter

Addie (center) and other missionaries as they leave San Francisco

29

Addie and missionaries on the ship to China

CHAPTER 6

LEARNING THE CHINESE LANGUAGE

As a youngster in Alabama, Addie naturally spoke English. Now she was in China and had to learn to speak Mandarin Chinese. In order to be able to talk with the boys and girls and with the Chinese people, it was necessary that she learn a new language — a very difficult language.

She was sent to language school in Peking, and in ten months she had mastered the Chinese language. It normally would have taken an average student two years to have a fair working knowledge of the language. Addie learned it in ten months. (Addie is really smart, isn't she?)

Addie wrote home to say that learning the Chinese language was no easy task. She said that in order to acquire the language, each word must have its proper tone or else one might find herself saying "pig" when she meant to say "Lord."

Another missionary said learning Chinese is work for men with bodies of brass, lungs of steel, eyes of eagles, hearts of apostles, memories of angels, and lives of Methuselah.

Not our Addie! After completing her language class, she spoke Chinese so well that she was selected to serve as acting principal of the girls' school at Kaifeng, China, capital of the Honan Province.

Hooray, for our Addie!

She is on her way as she begins her special contact with the Chinese people!

Embroidered
Chinese pagoda

Addie with other missionaries at language school

CHAPTER 7

TELLING THE CHINESE ABOUT JESUS

In School

At the girls' school, Addie did full-time school work, teaching all the organ and piano music with twelve pupils, teaching two Bible story classes a day, leading chapel services twice a week, teaching a Sunday school class, acting as Sunday school superintendent, and leading the Sunbeam Band (the group we now call Mission Friends). She tried to help every girl in the school to know about Jesus and His great love for them.

Addie talked with at least one student each afternoon about becoming a Christian, or, if the student was already a Christian, about growing in grace and winning others to Jesus.

She loved the school and the students, but she hoped that other teachers would come the next year and replace her at the school and give her the opportunity to devote all her time to evangelistic work.

In Preaching

Addie spoke of her love to tell others about Jesus as her "call." She understood that millions of people in China had never heard of Jesus, and she wanted to go and tell them "to go and preach" as she called it.

At that time, single women did not travel alone. It was dangerous, but it also was not the proper thing to do. Most women traveled with a Chinese "Bible woman," a Chinese woman believer in Jesus who knew the customs and ways of the Chinese people. Such Chinese women were a helpmate and extremely important to the work of the missionaries in sharing about Jesus. Addie's church in Alabama sent money to her each month to help with the expense of her "Bible woman."

One thing that missionaries had to do in China was convince the people that they loved them and only wanted to share the love of God with them. Many Chinese people believed that the main object of missionaries was to "decoy" children into the schools and chapels in order to take out the hearts and eyes of the children to be used in making medicine. The Chinese people also said that those who followed the "foreign devils," (a name they called our missionaries) would be given medicine that would cause them to "lay eggs" and eventually result in their death.

Addie told of one little boy who watched her eat supper, as did the children as they were lined up on benches around the table. "What is that yellow stuff?" asked the child. "This is butter," Addie replied ("yellow oil," in Chinese). The Chinese did not have butter, and the child had never seen any before. Speaking in an undertone, he said to the boy sitting by him, "Is that yellow oil made of little children?" Addie heard the whisper and assured him that the "yellow oil" was made from cow's milk and that he had nothing to fear.

In later years, Addie served in Taiwan when the missionaries were forced to leave the Chinese mainland. Addie worked with a small newly formed church, living simply in one room, as she visited, evangelized, and taught the Chinese. (Eating the food she prepared was a challenge. A breakfast of tomatoes, a few greens, and eggs broken into boiling water was her usual diet.) After other missionaries came into the area, Addie was assigned to northern Taiwan to begin new mission work there.

Addie working with small Chinese children

*Invitation to
Chinese Bible class*

英文查經班

歡迎參加！

時 間：每星期日上午九時
地 點：桃園中華路浸信會

**INVITATION TO ENGLISH
BIBLE CLASS EVERY SUNDAY
9:00 A.M., BAPTIST CHURCH**

Kaeling Baptist Church group, organized Oct. 29, 1951

Map showing locations of mission work in China

CHAPTER 8

TRAVELING TO SHARE GOD'S WORD

Travel for the missionaries in China was quite different from our travel today. Addie and other missionaries walked, ran, used bicycles, carts, "peace carts," wheelbarrows, horses, mules, wagons and Pekinese carts and chairs borne by four men. Oxen, cows, mules, horses and donkeys were used to pull the peace carts, and sometimes there were teams of four animals — one cow, one horse, one ox and one donkey — all used at the same time.

Occasionally, people rode the donkeys using wooden saddles. Addie said that riding the donkey with a wooden saddle was delightful when the donkey was galloping and she was in the air, but contact with the saddle was a disagreeable moment.

Sometimes they were in open carts when

the rain began. They covered themselves with whatever they had — maybe an umbrella, oil-cloth or rug — but many times the rain continued, and they and all their possessions were wet.

One time Addie rode in a Pekinese cart with a group of soldiers who were guarding her from robbers in the vicinity. These soldiers were ready to listen to the Gospel message, and they learned several Scripture verses and songs as they traveled on the long, sandy road. Danger from bandits had brought an opportunity for Addie to tell the story of Jesus and His love to the soldiers.

Addie said many people asked her, "Why did you come to this strange land?" She said it was because there were so many there who needed to know Jesus and have His peace and joy in their hearts.

At one village she was sharing about Jesus. The people listened as she taught them Bible verses and songs. They memorized the verses and songs. Then they said, "Please repeat it slowly, and let this young man write it down. There is no one here to teach us and when you go away; we may forget." The young soldier came and carefully wrote out the characters with his Chinese brush.

Can you imagine a whole village (maybe we would call it a small town) where there would not be even one copy of God's Word and no one to teach the people about its precious truths?

Addie with a Chinese church group

A Chinese statesman welcoming WMU Secretary Kathleen Mallory in 1923

Addie with a group of Chinese boys

44

CHAPTER 9

BICYCLES AND THE "GOSPEL FORD"

W. Carl Hunker, a young missionary, thirty years old, was on his way to China on December 15, 1946, with his wife, Jeanette, and their eighteen-month-old son, David. He tells us about meeting with Addie.

"The big ship was the Marine Lynx, a ship used by the military during World War I to carry soldiers. It was steel gray in color and certainly not equipped for the comfort of passengers. It was a gray, dark day when the ship left San Francisco to sail through the Pacific Ocean to Shanghai, China, on a sixteen-day trip."

Of the 970 passengers, 650 were missionaries and their children. Many were young missionaries leaving America for the first time, as the Hunkers were. Of this number, fourteen were Southern Baptist missionaries, and they had fourteen children with them.

The dining room on the ship was a typical military "mess hall." As Mr. Carl occasionally passed through the mess hall, he saw a short, stocky woman wearing a green visor to shade her eyes often sitting at one of the long tables. Addie was busy typing on the typewriter she carried with her. One day, Mr. Carl disturbed her by introducing himself and asking her where she was going in China.

Addie had already served in China for over twenty-five years. As Mr. Carl and his wife had no idea what supplies they needed to take to the mission field, he stopped to ask Miss Cox what she was taking. She told them she was taking a lot of things, including sixteen bicycles.

How amazing! He was embarrassed that he and his wife were taking only three bicycles — one for each of them and one for their son to ride as soon as he was old enough. He asked Addie why she was carrying so many. She explained that she would be giving the bicycles to country pastors, who had to walk long distances to their churches and chapels. Bicycles were the best way the pastors had to travel from their homes to the churches.

Addie also told the Hunkers she was keeping one bicycle for herself, as she otherwise would have to walk or run to her various meetings.

About a year later, at a missionary prayer meeting in Shanghai, Mr. Carl met Miss Cox again, a bit surprised that she had come all the way from Kaifeng. He learned that the communist armies had taken her area and were restricting church work. He was still curious about those sixteen bicycles. She was so happy to tell how grateful the pastors were when she gave them the bicycles.

Then Addie told Mr. Carl about the communist soldiers coming to her little hut and demanding that she give her bicycle to them. She looked at them sternly as she refused to give to them. "This bicycle was given to me to preach the good news of God. Are you going to preach about God?" They were startled by her refusal and replied with a timid "No."

"Then you can't have it. It's for God's work." The group of soldiers left without the bicycle.

We have all heard about the "Gospel Ford," but we have not found the facts on it. Whether this is the car that Alabama WMU gave Addie in 1928 for her work in China or whether it was another automobile given to her by her church in later years, we are not sure. We do know that Carrollton Baptist Church WMU contributed $600 toward the car given to her by the state WMU. We also know that Addie didn't drive, so someone else would have driven the car. But we have no trouble imagining her hopping into the Gospel Ford to go preaching — whether here in the homeland or there in China.

An early 20th-century bicycle similar to Addie's

A 1946 Ford similar to Addie's

CHAPTER 10

CUSTOMS THAT MADE ADDIE SAD

Customs are the practices of a people group that distinguish the group and set it apart from other people groups.

As much as Addie loved the Chinese people, there were customs of these people in the early part of the 1900s that made Addie's heart very sad.

One such custom was the neglect and abuse of baby girls in a family. A baby boy was a happy event for a home, but girls born into a non-Christian home were not always wanted. Girls were not valued among the Chinese people back then, and many times they were given away or sold. Sometimes they were even left on the streets without care. Often, Christian believers would take the abandoned baby girls into their homes and make them a part of their families.

Another practice was that of binding the feet

of a small girl child. A mother would bend the toes of her young daughter under her feet and keep them tightly bound so that her feet would grow that way. Many times this caused the feet to become sore and infected and would prevent the child from being able to walk, sometimes even when they were much older.

Christian schools began to refuse to accept students whose feet were bound or had been bound. Parents began to stop the practice of binding their daughters' feet so that they might be allowed to go to these schools that were so highly favored. We can be thankful that early missionaries did much to help the Chinese people stop these sad practices.

Shoes worn by little girls to bind their feet

Chinese women with bound feet

CHAPTER 11

ADDIE'S SENSE OF HUMOR

Addie had a great sense of humor, which helped her to face many of the hardships that she and other missionaries experienced. This was a special gift. She told many stories, including one about riding in a wheelbarrow.

Addie explained that in riding in the wheelbarrow, almost anything that might make it more comfortable for the rider caused a problem for the "barrow man." If one sits on a roll of bedding or something a bit elevated, the barrow man will say, "Your head is too high, I cannot see the road." If an umbrella is used to shade the eyes from the burning sun, he is likely say, "Your umbrella is too large. I cannot see." If a suitcase is placed so as to give the back support, he says, "The back is too heavy for the front. I'll just put this suitcase before you to make an even balance."

She also explained that the "peace cart"

often used for travel was evidently named by an optimistic person, for it was a four-wheel, springless wagon that jarred every nerve and muscle from the crown of the head to the sole of the foot.

Addie also talked about the curiosity that the Chinese women had about her. One day in a village meeting, during the prayer, while Addie's head was bowed, she felt someone tugging at her clothes. When she looked down, a woman was examining her clothes — both outer and inner. Addie gave the lady "a little tap to apprise her that someone was inside the clothes, but she calmly continued her examination." Addie then told the lady to listen to the message that was being shared about Jesus, but the lady said, "I never saw clothes like these before, so I wanted to look at them."

Another time as Addie traveled, she was riding in a rickshaw and, as usual, was talking to the rickshaw coolie about salvation in Jesus. He listened and showed great interest in what Addie was telling him. Addie began to hope that he would understand and be converted, as other rickshaw boys had been. But when she arrived at home and reached into her coin bag to pay the man, he said,

"I think the honorable lady should give me more than the usual price, because I listened so well to your preaching."

The rickshaw was used as early Chinese transportation

CHAPTER 12

CHINESE FRIENDS

Addie must have had many friends in China, but we know personally about Peter Tang, (whose last name was pronounced "Tong.")

Addie won Peter Tang to Christ. She gave us a little history on Peter's life. He was a captain in the army when God called him to preach in 1951. Peter was sure it would be impossible for him to be released from the military in order to go to seminary to study the Bible. But he prayed, and when God answered his prayer, he said, "The Lord has performed a miracle for me."

When this happened, he had been out of school for twelve years and had not finished high school or college. He knew it would be hard to go to seminary and study the Bible, but again he prayed, and God answered. He was accepted at the seminary in Formosa as a student on probation. This meant that he could go to the seminary as long as he made passing grades.

The school went even further to help Peter. He and other students who were unable to pay for their room, board and extra items were given work to do by the school. He was assigned fifteen hours a week writing and mimeographing in connection with translating books. Those extra hours, along with the hours that Peter studied, often kept him up late at night, but he worked hard and completed his work and study.

Peter came to Carrollton, Alabama, to visit Addie on one occasion. They went to prayer meeting at Addie's home church, where Peter gave a Gospel message.

Molly Clippard of Tuscaloosa, a close friend of Miss Addie and of Peter, sent a letter to the church after Addie's death; enclosed in the letter were two checks. The checks were to be used for the memorial marker for Miss Addie's grave — one check from Molly, and the other from Peter, who was at that time pastor of a Baptist church in Hong Kong.

On another occasion after Addie's death, Molly and Peter came to Carrollton to visit Addie's grave. After walking around in the cemetery, Molly came back and found Peter standing by Addie's grave, weeping like a little child. Peter Tang's transformed life, and his love and devotion to Addie, tells us that Addie was very special to the people she met in China.

Another man from China came and visited in Addie's church in Carrollton on two occasions. This man was Dr. Philip Xu, whose father helped Addie in telling others about Jesus in China. Philip told of a time when Addie and other missionaries gave his daddy ten eggs each day to help him cure his tuberculosis, a very serious illness. That may not seem like much to us today, because we have penicillin and other medicine, but Mr. Xu's family did not have the proper medicine, and those eggs from Addie's group may have been all they had each day.

Philip visited two times in Carrollton Baptist Church. The first time he came, he was in nursing training in Mobile. He remembered that Addie was from Alabama, and he began to search for her family. He gathered information from Washington that helped him locate the Cox family in Carrollton. He came to church on a Sunday morning and introduced himself to our pastor and members.

Several years later, after he had moved to Las Vegas, Nevada, and was serving as director of the university's nursing school, he came back to Carrollton and brought his mother (who still lived in China) to introduce her to the Coxes and to Addie's church. They wanted to see where Addie had lived and where she was buried in the city cemetery. They carried a beautiful bouquet of flowers and placed them on her grave. They spent the night in Lydia House, the church's missionary guest house, before continuing on to see Frances Cox Jones and her family in south Alabama.

A few years after Philip visited us for the last time, we learned that he had cancer and needed our special prayers. By this time I was regularly writing to him by email. One day I told him that I wanted to speak to him as I thought Addie would have spoken to him. I asked, "Philip, have you given your heart to Jesus and asked Him to be your Savior?" It was sad to hear Philip say that he had not yet asked Jesus into his heart but that he was studying about it. He explained that, having been reared in a Chinese home, it was more difficult for him to give up the beliefs that he had learned. I assured him that his friends in the United States would be praying for him to make this important decision. He thanked me.

We never knew the answer to that prayer, but we are hopeful that during his last days, as he knew that life was short, he seriously considered the consequences of his decision about whether or not to accept Christ.

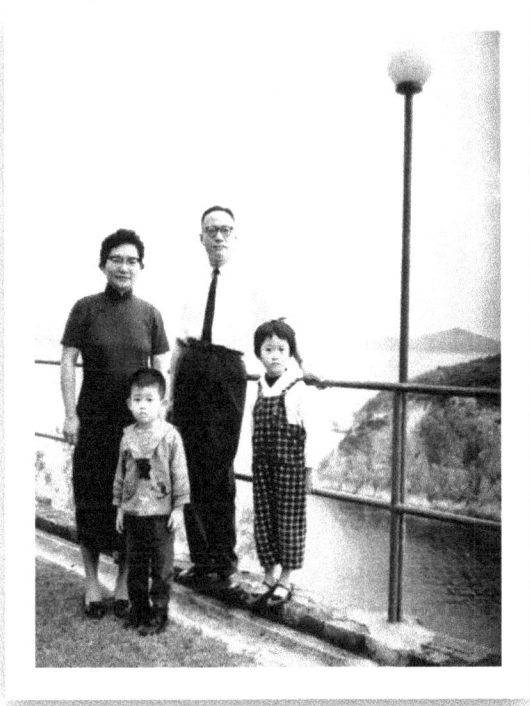

Peter Tang with family: wife, daughter Addie Cox, and son Billy Graham

Addie welcomed by Soong Mei-ling (Madam Chiang Kai-shek)

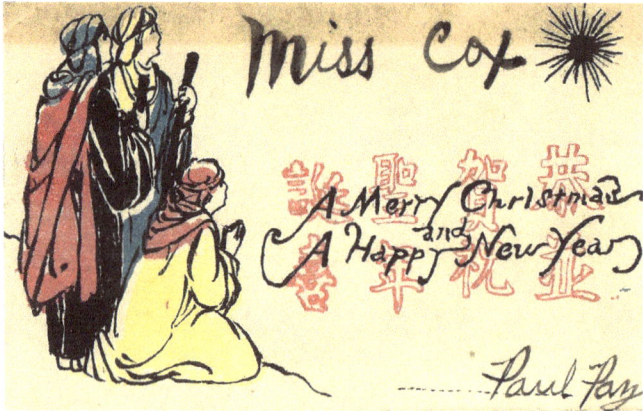

A Christmas card from a friend

64

Philip Xu with family: his father (on first row),
who helped Addie with mission work

Jeanne and Pastor Styles, Marie and Bootie Cox,
Mrs. Xu and Philip Xu place flowers on Addie's grave

CHAPTER 13

ADDIE'S POETRY

Addie liked poetry. She read it, she wrote it, and she was always sharing words written by herself or by others she appreciated.

One of her poems was a prayer speaking of God's care for her family far away in America. Writing those words in a prayer to God brought comfort to Addie, as she talked with Him and thought of her family. This poem was written in March 1922 in Kaifeng, Honan Province, China:

A Message to Loved Ones

On a clear, cold night
As I watched the brilliant signals above,
Flashing and sparkling their message,
"God is love,"

I thanked Him from the depths of my heart
For the marvelous and inspiring sight,
Filling my soul with wonder
And praise and delight.

"O, Beautiful Star,"
I said to one that seemed so near,
"This message for my loved ones
In far-off America, please hear,

And deliver to them at night:
'Though thousands of miles apart,
I love you with the deepest,
Tenderest devotion of my heart.'"

And, little Star, will you give
To each a kiss for me,
And say very gently, but definitely,
She prays for thee."

"Ah, child of His care"
Was the shining star's very wise reply,
"They are now within sight
Of our Father's ever watchful eye."

"It is true, my lovely Friend"
Was the answer I promptly made,
And thus to the Father Himself
I ardently prayed:

"I know Thou seest my dear ones
And knowest their ever need,
Bless them, O Father,
Let them live in Thy love, I plead."

"May Thy richest, fullest, sweetest
Blessings to them abound;
May they in Thy kingdom
And Thy service ever be found.

May they realize my love for them, too.
Do Thou guard them from every ill.
And in them work out
Thy holy and righteous will."

For Jesus' sake, Amen.

— Addie

Another poem I know you will like is:

A Shower

It comes from clouds you cannot see,
And yet they're bright as gold.
'Tis strong, but gentle as can be,
And tells a story old.

With ne'er a pause it falls all day,
At night 'tis falling still.
It has this sweet and constant way
An emblem to fulfill.

A peace it gives to many a heart,
As pure and fair as light;
They pray that it may ne'er depart
And turn their day to night.

But if there're those who do not know
The joy this shower brings,
They're sad and lone, their pulse is slow,
No song of gladness rings.

It does not fall from darkened sky
Or any place above
Its happy source is ever nigh:
It is … THE SHOWER OF LOVE.

— Addie Estelle Cox

CHAPTER 14

ADDIE'S SERVICE DURING WAR TIME

Addie went to China in July of 1918. She served in Kaifeng, China, until 1951 and served in Formosa the latter part of that year. She retired on October 24, 1955, and lived in Carrollton, Alabama, until her death on May 24, 1965.

Addie's first term of service was from 1918 to 1925 in Kaifeng. During her second term of service, from 1926 to 1934, she continued evangelistic work around Kaifeng. During the communist outbreak in 1927, she was compelled to leave the interior and live in coastal cities for ten months.

Her third term, from 1935 to 1944, was filled with war, flood, famine, bombings — and with seen and unseen; but the Lord was with her and protected her. She was able to continue her work and to do relief for flood refugees. Many of those refugees asked Addie questions about Jesus. Those questions helped to tell the story of Jesus to many people during the six years that the Japanese were on the east side of the Yellow River and Addie was just across on the west side in the area that was called "Free China."

The flood-sufferers came to her and other Christians for food, clothing, and shelter. God answered prayers from them over and over. There were more than 1,000 Chinese people, 800 of whom were living in their outstation mission compounds at one time. They were all being taught God's word day by day, in school and classes. During this period, several new churches were organized, a new association was organized, and a pastor was ordained.

Dishes representative of those left by communist soldier

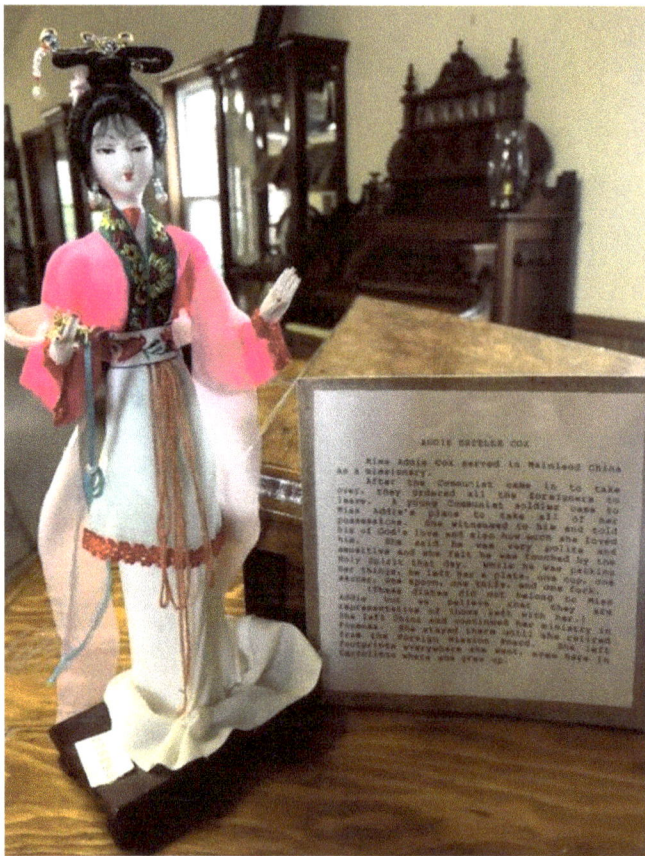

Chinese doll and explanation for the dishes

CHAPTER 15

ADDIE COMES HOME

Addie came back to her home in Carrollton, Alabama, and officially retired on October 24, 1955. As with many people who are dedicated to God's work in their lives, Addie did not sit at home in a rocking chair.

She visited prisoners at the county jail, often taking with her a great nephew, David Cox, and two neighbors, Bill Curry and Cary Alexander. The boys were youngsters, and it was a very special time for them to go to the jail with her to visit.

Her great niece Carolyn Cox Durel reminded me that Addie walked at a brisk clip, like many of the Chinese people. She also shared how Addie helped the grandchildren learn Scripture. Upstairs in Addie's room, she would give them a penny to quote a Scripture verse. They would run back downstairs, learn another verse, and run back upstairs to get another penny. The game ended suddenly one day when Addie caught them out on the porch throwing their pennies to the ground. Addie was so very disappointed.

Addie's sisters, Clara and Patty, moved back to the home in Carrollton after their husbands died. Addie invited her sisters and the grandchildren to have evening vespers in her room. This was a time of shared prayer and Bible reading, and it was a special time for all of them.

She also went to California to work with Chinese immigrants there. The love of God for the Chinese people was very strong in her heart. Since she was unable to go back to China, she would do the next best thing: minister to the Chinese people living in her own country.

As her health failed, she entered a nursing home in Tuscaloosa. There she continued to think of herself as a missionary as she told others about Jesus and His love.

Addie Cox

Addie and friends

CHAPTER 16

HONORED BY FAMILY AND FRIENDS

Addie's family, friends, and church supported her during the years she served in China.

After seven years on the field in China, Addie took her first furlough (visit home). It was great that she was in Carrollton at the same time the church's centennial anniversary was held on May 26, 1946. She was the main speaker that morning. It must have been a grand occasion to have Addie back for a visit and to have guests, former pastors, and former members to join the local church family in celebration of 100 years as they looked back over those years — not boastfully, but humbly and gratefully.

When Addie celebrated her seventy-first birthday, she was honored by her church with a surprise birthday party, complete with cake, gifts, and best wishes. The party was held one week early because Addie was scheduled to be out of town on her birthday working with the Home Mission Board in Montgomery, Alabama, as well as in Georgia and Tennessee. The church held an Addie Cox Missions Festival, sponsored by the Pickens Baptist Association, under the leadership of Dr. Gary E. Farley. A team of journalists from the International Mission Board came to cover the event in view of publishing the story in The Commission, the Southern Baptist mission magazine, in March 2000.

Members of the Cox family, along with friends, gathered for this special event. Many shared stories of her life and the profound influence Addie had on their lives. Dr. Farley said there were probably hundreds of people who had developed a heart for mission because of Addie Cox. He went on to say, "When I was growing up, not only did we eat for China ('Starving children in China would be glad to have those peas!'), but in our minds China was the image we had when we thought of missions and missionaries."

Among the guests were Anne Williams Faulkner and her husband, John Faulkner, retired Foreign Mission Board missionaries to Eastern and Southern Africa. Anne's home church, Springhill Baptist Church about ten miles west of Carrollton, was where Anne met Addie. Anne was among the youngsters who met Addie during her teen years and heard of her passion for missions. God used these times to influence Anne's call from Pickens County for overseas missions.

In the afternoon, Dr. Farley led a historical walk from the church past Addie's home place and on to her gravesite. A snack supper featuring Chinese food was held after the walk, and children as well as adults had fun using chopsticks for the first time.

Other mission guests included Gwen and Floyd Cooper from Mississippi. Mrs. Cooper was born in China, the daughter of Southern Baptist missionaries during the time that Addie was serving there.

Closing special music was given by Suzanne Smith, a pastor's daughter from the association, who sang "My House Is Full, But My Fields Are Empty." The song brought to our minds the same words that Addie often used.

Another time of celebration for Addie was held when a close friend of hers, Elizabeth Colvin, who had moved away from Carrollton, sent money for flowers for Addie's grave on her birthday. A special recognition was made in the morning worship service. Afterward, a small group led by the pastor went to the cemetery to place the flowers on her grave and to have a prayer.

Addie at the home of Mrs. Ida Stinson
in Alabama

100th anniversary of Carrollton Baptist, May 26, 1946

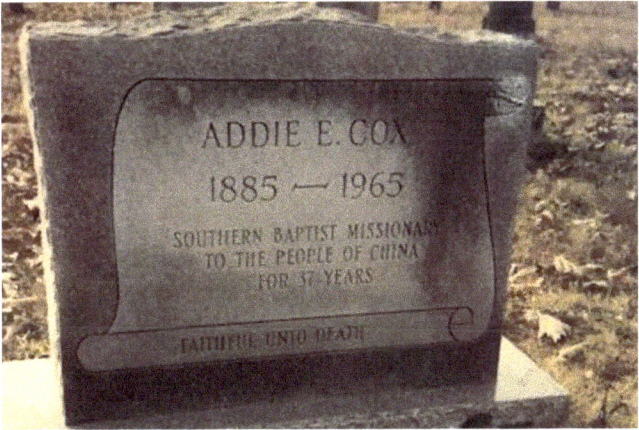

Addie's gravesite

85

Carrollton WMU honors Addie with flowers

Addie Cox Sunday School Class at Carrollton Baptist Church

Pickens Baptist Association children at Addie Cox Mission Day

ADDITIONAL PHOTOS

Addie dressed in Chinese attire

Addie tours an industrial plant

Addie and children on a camel at Sallee House,
where Addie lived in June 1920

Addie Cox and a missionary friend

Addie visits Cross Roads Baptist Church in Carrollton

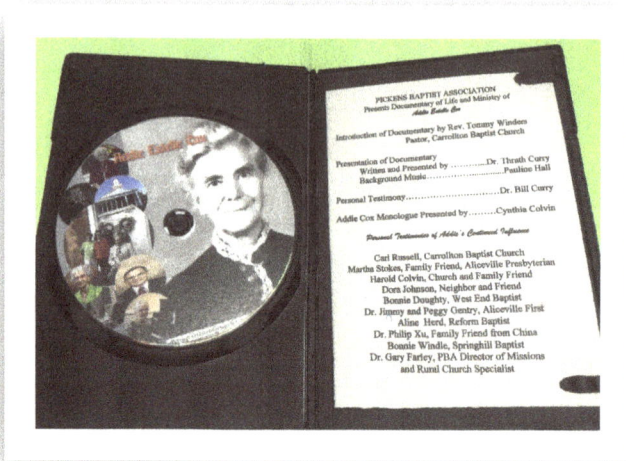

*Documentary on the life and work of Addie Cox
by Pickens Baptist Association*

Pickens Baptist Association group working on Addie's book

Appreciation

Many thanks to the Cox family for their help in gathering pictures and articles on Addie's life and work: her nephew, Clayton Cox, Jr. (whom we knew as Bootie) and his wife Marie; as well as their daughter Carolyn Cox Durel and their son Keith Cox; and Frances Cox Jones (Addie's niece) and her family.

In addition to the family, thanks go to church and association members for all their contributions. Especially helpful among this group was the Addie Cox Senior Adult Women's Sunday School Class at Carrollton Baptist Church, which I taught in the early 1970s. This class supported me in the dream of a curio cabinet for Addie's memorabilia to be displayed at the Pickens Baptist Association office. This dream grew to two cabinets — one at the association and one at our church.

Others who were a vital part of our work include Dr. Thrath Curry (a Sunday school teacher at Carrollton Baptist Church for over sixty years) and Dr. Gary Farley, associational director of missions. Dr. Curry, who wrote the documentary that was published by Pickens Baptist Association in 1999, was a next-door neighbor to Addie and knew her well. Others in the group led by Dr. Farley included Carl Russell, Marie Perkins, Dr. Jimmy and Peggy Gentry, Harold Colvin, Martha Haynie Stokes, Pauline Hall, Cynthia Colvin, Aline Herd, Dora Johnson, Bonnie Doughty, Philip Xu, Tommy Winders (pastor of Addie's home church), and myself.

Thanks also to my niece Teri Killough Chapman, of Colorado, who created the cover illustration for this book.

May those of us who knew Addie, and those who have learned about her life and work, renew the dedication of our lives to Christ, to whom Miss Addie gave a long and beautiful life of service and devotion.

— *Bonnie Gates Windle*

About the Author

Bonnie Gates Windle grew up in rural Alabama on a small family farm and learned early to love God's creation. Her favorite spot today is looking out her kitchen window at the dogs, cats, chickens, beautiful birds and the squirrels at play. That is where her desk is located and where she works and continues her reading through the Bible.

She has a strong love for God, family and people. Having had the opportunity to meet people in national settings, her worldview is broader than it might have been. She has been a passionate reader since she was twelve years old, and much of that reading has given her a greater love for God and for His mission work. Having spent over forty years in a legal office, she used most of her vacation time in mission work, often in Brazil, and other times in local and North American missions. The new federal women's prison in Aliceville, Alabama, has opened a new field of service for area residents, and she has been active in that work and hopes to continue to minister there.

She has two children, four grandchildren and two great-grandchildren. Having recently lost her husband of sixty-one years, she has entered a new phase of life and continues to seek God's direction.

www.ingramcontent.com/pod-product-compliance
Lightning Source LLC
LaVergne TN
LVHW010308070426
835511LV00022B/3466